P9-DMK-037

The Power of People:

Four Kinds of People Who Can Change Your Life©

Verna Cornelia Simmons, Ph.D.

JCAMA Publishers©

The Power of People:
Four Kinds of People Who Can Change Your Life©

©2002 by Verna Cornelia Simmons, Ph.D.

Published by JCAMA Publishers

Editor: Laura T. Young, M.S.
Cover Illustration and Design: Tee Simmons
Desktop Publisher: Marilyn Alstrup and Jane Ramseth
Publishing Consultant: Tami Rangel

All Rights Reserved. No part of this book may be reproduced or utilized in any form or by any means, electronic or mechanical, including photocopying, recording, or by any information storage or retrieval system, without permission in writing from the Publisher. Inquiries should be addressed to:

JCAMA Publishers
Robbinsdale, MN 55422
www.jcama.com

Simmons, Verna Cornelia, 1963-
The Power of People: Four Kinds of People
Who Can Change Your Life.

LCCN 2002110864
ISBN 0-9717765-0-4
Printed in U.S.A. on acid-free paper
Distributed by JCAMA Publishers

"Our deepest fear
is not
that we are inadequate.
Our deepest fear
is that
we are POWERFUL beyond measure"

-Nelson Mandela[1]

1 Mandela, N. (1994). [A 1994 inaugural speech, written by Marianne Williamson]. Http://www.lightshift.com/inspiration/mandela.html

TABLE OF CONTENTS

Thoughts For Readers

Each of us will come to a point in life when we realize we must change or else! These moments are often painful and intense. Welcome to humankind; you are not alone!

When I was in my early 30s, I had a revelation that God created me to be a powerful person who can change my world for the good. This revelation put me on a course to discover and pursue my personal purpose. I have found that when you begin to understand your personal power, you will not only change your life for the better, but most importantly, you will change your world in a positive way. I believe that everyone who reads this book and acts on its principles will never be the same. You will become a powerful person who is positively changing your life and your world. You will no longer wait for someone to lead you; you will become the ultimate personal leader.

In the moments you spend with this book, you can challenge yourself to change or you can remain in your comfort zone and miss an important opportunity to become your most excellent self! I have come to believe that your response to change and challenges is based on how much you know about your personal power, your personal purpose, and your power to influence and be influenced by others.

Having responded to difficult changes and challenging people in my own life, I encourage you to pursue your realization of a personal power with passion. I believe that your ultimate happiness and success in life is directly related to how you use your personal power. This book is a journey of understanding yourself, your purpose and your power to make changes in your life. Change is never easy. For that reason, many of the ideas and thoughts that you will encounter while reading this book will provoke and challenge you. Accept the challenge, change and begin to positively use your personal power. I know that you can change. I know that you are a powerful person.

Chapter 1

WHO ARE WE? WHO ARE YOU?

Where do we spend most of our time? For better or worse, it is with or around people. People are the foundation of our human existence. We need people to exist, to truly live, to love, and to dream. People are powerful. We are powerful forces of life who can and have moved civilizations to great innovations and progress and to incomprehensible demise. That is the power of people. Why are we so powerful? Very simple: God created people to be powerful. By giving us the most powerful tool known to humankind: the power of Choice. It amazes me that God could have created people to be robots to listen and obey His very command, but instead, gave people power to choose. That boggles my mind!

So you see, as people we are very powerful because we can choose. What does having choice mean? It means that we can change our lives. It also means that we can influence other people by the choices we make and the consequent actions we take. This is an awesome revelation! Why? Because the majority of people on this earth do not realize their own power to choose, power to change their lives, and power to influence others. As a result, people live lives of non-action, regret, bitterness, and idleness. In other words, some people can exist in this life but never begin to truly live because they never realize their power. What does this mean? It means that a person who doesn't realize his or her power to influence can still severely influence your life for better or worse. Some people are simply "wrecks" waiting to happen in *your* life. We need to be able to identify these people concretely and learn to help them realize their power to change or we need to *run* for our lives! On the other hand, there are also people waiting to be a blessing in your life, to help your life, and to increase your life. When you find people who understand their power to change themselves and influence their world, you must know how to keep them in your life. Why? Because they could be the exact influence that you need to help you be the powerful and purposeful person God created you to be.

In this book, we will explore four kinds of people, powerful people, who can and will change your life, if you let them. This book is designed to give you "on-time, just-in-time" information. Some of the practical examples will challenge you, and might even offend you. Keep reading. Why? Because there is a law of life: You will never change unless you are challenged. Never, Never, Never. So

> *You will never change unless you are challenged.*

if you are offended, I encourage you to **get over it!** Let yourself be challenged and begin to change.

I believe this book has been given to me to write because I firmly believe in the power of people. I want every person to realize his or her power and begin to use it positively to change themselves and those around them. Our world is severely in need of positive powerful people and I believe that you are one of those people.

WHO ARE WE ? WHO ARE YOU ?

Chapter 2

WHAT IS POWER?

Power as a concept is a loaded term. For many people, power is a negative term because it denotes issues of abuse, political corruption, an unjust society, or inequalities. Who do we view as powerful in our world? Mostly, it's the public, so-called leaders of countries and companies; famous people such as entertainers, writers, television personalities, and those considered wealthy. Most of us link the concept of power to money, position, or personal possessions. For example, many people consider a person like Bill Gates, the Microsoft guru, to be powerful. Why? Because he has lots of money, runs a huge company, and has tons of stuff.

Unfortunately, some people use their money, position, and stuff to make themselves feel powerful, but if it is taken away, they will self-destruct. Why? Because they never got a revelation about their personal power that transcends position, money, or stuff. More and more, I have begun to ask, "Who would I be without my stuff?" Does my stuff make me and control me or would I be just as powerful without the stuff? Do you know people who are absolutely controlled by stuff? They spend their time thinking about their stuff, they worry about their stuff, they get offended when someone else has better or more stuff. Who are you without your stuff? Yes, you can have cars, houses, clothes, vacations, money, and education, but if you are a person who lives an outwardly happy life but suffers silently, your stuff won't help you. We spend a lot of time in our society using our stuff to disguise our real pain and lack of personal power. It's time for that to change. Today!

So, what is power? Power has multiple definitions. Webster's Dictionary defines power from eight perspectives; I will focus on five.[2]

    ∞ Power is the "ability to do or act." That is, power enables us to make choices and make movement. It lends itself to adventure and creativity. Why? Because we can act; we don't have to sit by and let

> *Power is the "ability to do or act."*

things happen; we can do something about it. There is an epidemic in our world of helplessness and hopelessness. People exist an entire lifetime in a state of "Oh, me, oh, my" or "Oh, well" or "Well, you know, I'm only one person." People use excuses so they can feel better about their inaction mostly because they lack self confidence and knowledge about their personal power. They also make excuses out of fear.

∞ Power as "vigor, force, and strength" is the second definition. People who operate in their personal power have an abundance of energy for life. They have purpose and they have passion. Energy creates energy. As you realize your personal power and develop energy and vigor for life, you will automatically produce new levels of energy that will propel you forward as you seek to affect your community and world in a positive manner.

∞ One of my favorite definitions is power as a means of authority and influence. In other words, you know who you are, what you know and don't know, and what you can do. So, you operate with a sense of authority wherever you go. Later in the book, we will talk about how to take your environment with you. That is, how to establish instant authority and influence wherever you go.

∞ This definition expands on the previous one: Power is a person or thing having great influence, force, or authority. It's interesting that Webster's editors broke down this definition to point out that authority, influence, and force do not operate alone. These concepts can't exist without people, who give them dimension and effect. This aspect of power is based on relationships. The reality is that with out people and relationships, your power has no effect! You need power to influence others.

∞ Power is the result of multiplying a quantity by itself. Only when you realize your personal power can you begin to see the multiplication effect. Understanding how your life multiplies itself is imperative. People wonder why their lives don't get better; it's because their lives are constantly multiplying the negative. In contrast, if you are a positive person, you tend to have positive people, purpose, and goals in your life. These positives increase themselves as you realize your power to multiply.

You have power! Where is your power? In you. The way to access your power is to decide to be challenged and to change. You must change your mind, your relationships, and your actions.

---

2 Webster's New Collegiate Dictionary (1974). G & C Merriam Co.

Chapter 3

PURPOSE OF PERSONAL POWER

Purpose is critical to personal power. What is purpose? Many writers, including international figure Myles Munroe[3], point to the critical role of purpose in our lives. Know your purpose; that is, what you were created to do, who were you created to be, and what you were created to bring to others. You must ask yourself, "Why do I have personal power, and what am I supposed to use this power to do?" Not understanding their purpose is one important reason why people don't realize their power. To access the personal power stored in you, you must first grapple with these questions:

- Why do I want Power?
- Why do I have Power?
- Power for what?
- What will I accomplish with my Power?
- How will I influence my family, friends, community, society, and world

with my Power?

The bottom line is that you must know *why* you want personal power. In writing this book, I am aware of a potentially dangerous side effect of

> *you must know **why** you want personal power.*

teaching the concepts of power. Personal power can be used to do harm. I pray that as you read this book, you will understand clearly that my purpose in writing it is to empower people to discover and realize their personal power so that they can begin to create positive change in their world. Too many people have used their personal power negatively or wickedly. I believe that when you realize your personal power, your purpose must be to enhance, empower, and help others, not hurt them. I pray to God that you will use your power to help and not hurt because there is a law of God called, "seed, time, and harvest." In other words, whatever you do to others, will eventually be done to you.

The animated classic, *Toy Story*, is a great illustration of this law. In the story, the boy, Sid, used his personal power to destroy his toys. He did this for many years until he made the mistake of trying to destroy one of the lead characters, Buzz Light Year. When Woody, the other lead character, realized Sid's intentions, he used his personal power to create a plan to stop Sid and rescue Buzz. Woody talked with all the toys that Sid had hurt, and encouraged them to stand up to Sid. He helped them understand that they didn't have to put up with Sid's negative behavior anymore. They got motivated, tapped into their personal power, confronted Sid about his behavior and rescued Buzz. The movie ended when Woody designed a scheme to frighten Sid. Woody warned Sid to be good or the toys he treated badly would end up destroying him. Woody told Sid that if he continued using his power to hurt others, sooner or later, someone would use his/her power to hurt him.

Every time you use your personal power to help, you are preparing a good future for your life. If you use your personal power to hurt or destroy others, sooner or later you too will be destroyed. It is a law of life, *so do good!* Before you read on, you

> *Every time you use your personal power to help, you are preparing a good future for your life.*

must make up your mind and heart to use your personal power for good. Otherwise, please throw this book away, burn it, or give it to someone who will use it for good. I truly mean that.

---

[3] Munroe, Myles (1998). <u>Seasons of Change: Understanding Purpose in Times of Perplexity.</u> Pneuma Life Publishing: Lanham, MD

Chapter 4

WHO ARE THE POWERFUL PEOPLE IN YOUR LIFE?

Before you begin to read about the four types of powerful people who can affect your life, you must ask yourself, "Who are the powerful people in my life?" Who are the people, who have influenced me the most, positively or negatively? Be honest. *No*, you don't have to show anyone this list; it is your own personal work. But you must *be honest* and courageous enough to identify these people. Why? Because, as you begin to read about the four types of powerful people, you will want to ask, "How does this person influence my life, for the good, bad, or ugly?" Who is it, how does the person influence you, and very importantly, *why* are you influenced by them?

What does influence mean? It means asking whether this person's words, actions, or behaviors consistently:

⁓ cause you to think differently about your life in a significant way,

- affect the types of significant choices you are making in your life, or

- significantly affect your actions or behaviors. If you allow it, anyone can influence your life significantly.

"Just Is" People

We have two categories of people in our lives. The first group of people we did not choose, such as parents, siblings, and relatives. I call family members the "Just Is" people. Some people spend a whole lifetime wishing they had a different set of parents, siblings, and relatives. Also included in the "Just Is" people are spouses and children. Never regret your "Just Is" people! Learn to learn from them. Learn to think critically about what they teach you to do and not to do with your life. "Just Is" people are in our lives for a purpose. For some, your "Just Is" people have given

> *You don't have to be friends with your "Just Is" people; you only have to be respectful and kind!*

you nothing but heartache, pain, and misery. The key to living without regrets about your "Just Is" people is to ask yourself, "What have I learned?" You don't have to be friends with your "Just Is" people; you only have to be respectful and kind! That's it! The Holy Bible tells us, "Honor your mother and father," it doesn't say you must like them! As matter of fact, you don't even have to hang around them! For some of us, this is a *major revelation!*

"Choice" People

The other category consists of "Choice" People. These are people we choose as friends, mentors, acquaintances, or pastors. We cannot change the " Just Is" people so we must learn to understand how they influence our lives and choose whether we want them to become the "Choice" People. This exercise will be very painful and disturbing for some because it means that you will have to face some *realities*. For example, my realization that my parents were some of the most powerful and influential people in my life meant that I had to understand how and why they had such power.

Be honest; those who influence your life could include parents, spouses, friends, co-workers, pastors, mentors, even your children. A way to think about "Choice People" is to ask these questions:

- ∞ Who do I talk to most of the time about important life issues?
- ∞ Who do I spend most of my quality time with?
- ∞ Whose opinions do I respect, fear, or admire?
- ∞ When I need to make important decisions, whom do I consult?

Don't consider the order of the names or how many are on the list; just start writing. When you can no longer think of those who influence you, stop writing.

People Who Currently Influence My Life

∞ _____

_____

∞ _____

_____

∞ _____

_____

Chapter 5

HOW ARE POWERFUL PEOPLE INFLUENCING YOUR LIFE?

You just identified the powerful people who influence you. Now begin to think about *how* these people influence your life. Remember that influence can happen in multiple dimensions. People can influence you emotionally, spiritually, physically, and psychologically. For example, are you still influenced by your parents such that you constantly seek their approval about your life decisions, even though you are a Grown-up?

I am amazed by how many Grown-up children are still running to their parents for approval and affirmation. This has resulted in another revelation for me: "Just because you are a Grown-up, doesn't mean that you Grew Up." Growing up is much more than physical maturation; it requires that you also grow in every dimension of your life and that you realize your personal power. Unfortunately, many grown people who are seeking this parental approval will never get it; therefore, they live in the realm of "if only my parents would … ." Well, more than likely, your parents won't, so let it go and make a decision, a choice, to realize your personal power!

This may sound harsh but it is a reality.

> *Personal power is an internal, spiritual force within all of us that is simply waiting to be realized and used.*

Begin right now to *release* your parents and begin realizing your power! The amazing fact about personal power is that it has nothing to do with other people, including your parents. Personal power is an internal, spiritual force within all of us that is simply waiting to be realized and used. Yes, parents and others can encourage you to tap into your personal power, but it's something that *only you can do.*

This book is your document and it is between you and God, but if you never deal with the realities in your life, you will never realize personal power. That's a fact. How many people do you know who live in denial, live a lie, or live in La-La land? Recently, I heard a pastor articulate the definition of denial. She said, denial means: <u>D</u>on't <u>E</u>ven <u>K</u>now <u>I</u> <u>A</u>m <u>L</u>ying to myself![4] This cracked me up, because it was so simple, true, and profound! Get out of denial and face your realities.

Not long ago, I was invited to do some consulting at a conference at one of the Disney World resorts. My family and I decided to extend our stay into a vacation, a dream come true for our six-year-old son. Each morning, I would take a walk around the resort and stop to read my Bible, talk to God, and meditate. The resort was very clean and beautifully designed, with lovely landscapes, water streams, recreational facilities and walking paths. One morning, as I looked out at all of the early morning people taking walks, jogs, or enjoying meditation time, it occurred to me that this was a perfect sort of world that Disney had created. You had everything you needed, for a price, you could just pretend life was perfect. At that moment, I had a major revelation that this was indeed La-La land. This was not reality! Soon every person at the resort would have to leave the perfect place and go back to their neighborhoods, family, people, and jobs that were less than perfect and they would have to deal with their realities. I also became somewhat sad because I realized that many people live in their own personal La-La lands, pretending life is perfect because they do not want to deal with their realities.

Unfortunately, people who don't deal with their realities are never challenged and will never change. Every year, their lives remain the same or they get deeper into lives of lies and denial. These are often some of most bitter, sad, critical, and resentful people you will ever meet. They translate into what is known as "difficult people" who are hard to talk to, live with, and work with. Show me someone who is unwilling to deal with realities, and I will show you a powerless person. Why? Because our personal power is based on a foundation of dealing with realities. We make choices to change our realities and, in turn, change our lives. That's power. Some families have been denying their realities for generations. For example, some families refuse to deal with alcoholism or drug abuse and live a lie for an entire lifetime. In essence, they live in La-La land

when it comes to their family. They may not
want to believe or face the painful truth so they
just pretend that everything is okay. Deal with it,
whatever it is! Deal with it. Why? Because personal power is waiting for you on the other side
of choosing to deal with your realities.

How do people influence your life? They can
influence your way of thinking, your choice of
relationships, your self-esteem, your life attitudes,
major life decisions, how you treat others, and
how you relate to God. People can influence us
negatively or positively, so **be honest**! If you are
not honest, they could actively and negatively
influence your life forever! For example, when I
realized that I was socialized by some of my "just
is" to distrust and manipulate people, *Be bold,*
courageous,
and
honest!
I had to learn how to honor and
respect people because my powerful
childhood influences were actively influencing
my daily actions and attitudes as an adult. That
was a powerful and painful revelation. Be bold,
courageous, and honest! Write down the names
of people who have influenced your life in a
powerful way, then explain how. Below, I have

shared some of my real life examples to encourage you to begin writing.

Influential People
co "Just Is" -Close family member
How They Influence My Life
co Taught me not to trust people

Influential People
co Choice
How They Influence My Life
co Taught me to be excellent always

Influential People
co My First Boss
How They Influence My Life
Taught me to be honest but kind

Now It's Your Turn. Remember to *be honest*!

HOW ARE POWERFUL PEOPLE INFLUENCING YOUR LIFE?

Influential People

∞ _____

_____

∞ _____

_____

∞ _____

_____

How They Influence My Life

∞ _____

_____

∞ _____

_____

∞ _____

_____

---

[4] Bishop Barbara Amos (2001), E.C. Reems International Women's Conference, Houston, Texas.

Chapter 6

THE ADDERS IN YOUR LIFE

Powerful people are those who add to your life. They are known as Adders. How can you identify an Adder? It's as simple as elementary school math. One of the first things young children learn in school is that 1 + 1 = 2. This might seem simple but it is a core principle of powerful people. Adders bring positive influence into your life without attaching strings. They add to your life not for self-gratification, self-promotion, or to use you but because they authentically care about you as a person and want to empower you to reach your fullest potential. The heart of an Adder is to see you become a positive, powerful person.

Adders can sometimes seem nosey or even invasive because they tend to ask lots of questions. They really want to know more about you so they can add to the areas of your life that might be lacking. Adders are interested in helping you become a whole, well-rounded, balanced person. For example, some people are so introverted and shy they won't say a word around others. Trying to have a conversation with them is almost painful because you feel as though you are constantly pulling on them to speak or that you are talking to a wall. On the other hand, some people are so extroverted and talkative that they rarely stop to listen to anyone else because they are too busy trying to be the center of attention and control the conversation.

When an Adder sees areas in your life that are missing, lacking, or extreme, they will work with you to increase or change those problems. Let me warn you that having an Adder in your life is not always comfortable. Adders can appear to be judgmental because they point out problems to you. Allowing Adders to influence you requires humility because you must understand what needs to be added before an Adder can be helpful to you. For example, I am working on becoming a more gentle and graceful person. So, I look for people, particularly women, who are gentle and graceful and who can add to my life.

What Gets Added To Your Life?

Adders can add to your life in many ways. They add to your confidence by affirming your gifts, talents, and abilities. They help you understand and appreciate how much you have to offer your world. Adders always try to help you grow and mature. True Adders try to get you to think about what you have to give first, then they help

Adders always try to help you grow and mature.

you increase what you have to give. For example, if you are a good communicator, an Adder will help you become a better communicator.

People who have Adders in their lives stay confident in who they are and what they have to offer society.

Adders help you increase your determination. Adders are great encouragers. They are not in your life to take from you so they often give selflessly so that you can increase and prosper. Adders refuse to listen to you complain, without reminding you of your life goals, your talents, and your abilities. Sometimes, Adders can be very tough on you. They don't need to be touchy, feely, "Oh, poor baby" types, but they will care enough about you to tell you the truth and encourage you to progress. The attitude of Adders is "It's not about me." Adders understand that we are on this earth to serve others, to increase the lives of others, and to help others realize their personal power. The goal of an Adder is to help you realize who you are, what you have to offer, and what you need to change so you can grow up and be the powerful person you were created to be. Adders don't have to be your closest friends, but they must be in your life if you want to increase.

Power Of Words

Adders understand the power of words. They understand that you are your greatest prophet. Whatever you say about yourself is what you will become. It is a law of life. If you speak negatively about who you are, "I'll Never, I Can't" that's exactly what you will do. Adders do not tolerate negative words that decrease your life. You can always tell when Adders are present because the moment you speak negatively about yourself or others, Adders try to make you see the positive side. Sometimes, Adders appear angry or irritated when they listen to you speak negatively because they understand what your words will do to you and they know that their goal is to bring positive, life-enhancing words to you. Now, don't be fooled. Adders know the difference between reality and fantasy. They correct you if you are living in La-La land, refusing to deal with your real life. For example, some people lie about their accomplishments and abilities. If you find yourself exaggerating often, you are lying. Why do you need to inflate your stories or your accomplishments? Is it to make yourself look better? People who brag are usually trying to cover up inadequacies or their low self-esteem. Adders call you on your stories and help you to be realistic about who you are.

Adders encourage you to change and offer to help you change. Many people don't realize their bosses are Adders. When their bosses point out problems that need work, these people get an "Attitude," and forfeit an opportunity for their bosses to add to their lives.

Here is a warning that could keep you from chasing Adders out of your life. If someone sees potential in you and points out areas that you need to work on, instead of getting an attitude, say *thank you*! Then, proceed to work on the problem. If you don't know how to work on that area, ask and s(he) might even provide you with the resources you need. But, if you get an attitude, you can forget it. An attitude is a clear sign that you are not humble enough to learn anything from anybody. It signals that you think you already know it all. I am amazed by people who, when asked or confronted about an issue, respond with, "I know that." Well, if you know it, then *do it!*

Adders are very careful about the words they use because they understand that words can encourage or discourage, build up or destroy you. For example, I believe that teachers are very powerful people. I have observed how teachers use words to encourage children to learn or destroy their confidence and willingness to

> *Adders are very careful about the words they use because they understand that words can encourage or discourage, build up or destroy you.*

learn. I remember one classroom where a student walked up to a teacher with a book and the teacher immediately responded, "You don't think you could read *that* book do you?" With that one statement, the boy's confidence to read that book was stripped from him. The boy's shoulders fell, his facial expression became a frown, and he walked back to his seat with one of the most helpless, dejected looks I've ever seen. His willingness to read and learn had been destroyed by one sentence from a powerful person. Within moments, the boy developed a behavior problem in the class, and shortly after, the teacher sent him out of the classroom. The teacher hadn't been careful with her words, wasn't aware of the power of her words, and wasn't conscious of how her power was affecting the lives of children. Adders watch what they say and listen carefully to the words of others. They know that it is in our words that we create our future.

Power Of Time

Adders are very aware of the power of time. They are goal-driven, destiny-oriented, purpose-minded people who understand that we all have only so many years to create positive change in our world. Therefore, they are careful with how they use time, who uses their time, and how to make time work for them. Adders are busy people, who are involved in community change and personal change simultaneously. The goal of an Adder is to bring or give something new to your world. They are hard-working people who are always on the lookout for others who are purpose-driven and destiny-driven. Adders realize that people who have a sense of vision and destiny are those who allow someone else to add to their lives. They have something Adders need and want to accomplish.

Adders challenge you to analyze how you use your time. They realize that whatever you make a habit will become a lifestyle and eventually your destiny. Some years ago, I was thoroughly convinced at a women's retreat when the speaker said, "You are living your priorities." She made it clear that how we use our time determines what we value in our lives. Adders clearly know that all people, regardless of culture,
ethnicity, religious, or socioeconomic status are

given two very important powerful gifts: the gift of time and the gift of choice. If you aren't willing to change how you use your time, it will be difficult to change your life. Adders work to help you use your time wisely; they ask you questions about why you do certain things habitually. For example, I am perplexed by the number of hours people watch television. How many people do you know who come home from work and watch four or five hours of television? For what? What do they learn from those hours of sitting and watching the screen? How is television adding to your life? Have we become a nation of letting others work hard and succeed while we sit and watch and not grow, mature, or change? If you are to change your life, you must change how you use your time. Remember, energy creates energy. Adders realize that when you begin to change how you use time, you will gain momentum, and before you know it, your life will begin to increase and prosper.

Power Of Knowledge

Adders constantly offer you opportunities to gain new knowledge, education and wisdom.

They are constantly learning something new that will enhance their lives. In learning and applying new knowledge, we grow, mature, and begin to fulfill our potential. Adders challenge you: to think a new thought, to learn about a new topic, to read a new book, to research a new topic, to seek a broader educational path. Knowledge and its application are key to realizing your power. Powerful people are knowledgeable, informed, and educated people. You must learn something new if you are to realize your power. Adders understand that their minds are powerful and capable of phenomenal understanding and wisdom. You must be determined to acquire new knowledge; you can go only as far as the information in your brain.

Powerful people are knowledgeable, informed, and educated people.

Learn something new, think about it, and apply it. Adders may give you a new book to read, advise you to attend a seminar, or encourage you to listen to informational tapes. They are interested only in adding to your knowledge base. Adders realize that if you learn something new, you will challenge yourself to grow and

34

mature in new ways.

Remember, the goal of an Adder is to bring increases to your life. I am blessed to have a number of Adders in my life. One particular person continually adds to my life by providing me with new books about leadership and success. Every time I am around her, I can count on hearing about a new book, a new tape, or a new speaker. I always leave her presence with opportunities for increase in my life. Why do I say opportunities? Adders can't force you to want to increase your life. Their role is to provide you with the opportunities to learn, grow, mature, and change. If you choose not to read the books, listen to tapes, heed their counsel, or act on the influence they offer, it's your loss!

You must choose to have Adders at work in your life. Adders can't and won't force you to change. I have found that it's best to act on whatever an Adder brings to my life because it's always for the good. Recently, I was consulting with a local urban high school that had undergone difficult times with the community, students, teachers, and administration. I pointed out to the new principal that it was very important for him to honor the work that his teachers and staff had done to bring about positive change in the school. I warned him that if he was not knowledgeable about the school's mission, goals, and vision that already existed and did not publicly honor the teachers and staff for that work, he would immediately lose their respect and lose his ability to be viewed as a leader in that school. He realized immediately that I was adding to his potential to be a powerful person in that school and responded, "You are a very good coach; I will do that, thanks." The principal could have said, "Yeah, yeah, I know that," gotten an attitude and lost the opportunity to enhance his leadership. The point is that Adders hope that you will gain new knowledge and apply it to help you uncover the powerful person who is within you.

What Happens To You When You Have Adders In Your Life?

Here are some ways to know whether Adders are contributing to your life.

> ∽ You gain a new sense of confidence in your skills, talents, and abilities.

- ❦ You gain access to new knowledge, information, and education.
- ❦ Your self-esteem increases.
- ❦ You begin to dream again; you may even discover a vision for your life.
- ❦ Your attitude about your life and your future is positive and hopeful.
- ❦ You have an overall sense of happiness, peace, joy, and fulfillment.
- ❦ You begin to evaluate who the Adders are in your life.
- ❦ You begin to discover new resources that can increase your life.
- ❦ You begin to think about yourself as a powerful person, who can positively change your world.
- ❦ You become an Adder yourself.

Now, think about the influential people who are currently in your life. Go back and look at your list. Now, be honest; are any of these people Adders? Why? How are they adding to your life? How are they causing your life to increase? How are they helping you to realize your potential, find a balance in life, and become a powerful person? How are they helping you create positive change in your world? *Be honest*! If you don't have any people on your list who are Adders, take a giant personal-growth step and make a declaration to yourself that you will become an Adder to others and that you will seek Adders for your life. Look at your Influential People list again and think about how many of those people are adding to your life. Then think about *how* they are adding to you life. Now, please write down your thoughts.

Who Are Adders In My Life?

∞ _____

_____

∞ _____

_____

∞ _____

_____

THE POWER OF PEOPLE

How Do they Add to my Life?

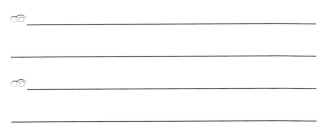

_____

_____

_____

_____

_____

_____

I believe that as we discover our personal power, we should all be Adders. Take a moment to think about and write down whose life you are adding to and how.

Whose Life Am I Adding to?

_____

_____

_____

_____

THE ADDERS IN YOUR LIFE

_____

_____

How Do I Add to His or Her Life?

_____

_____

_____

_____

_____

_____

Chapter 7

THE SUBTRACTERS IN YOUR LIFE

Life for the Subtracter is based on a foundation that says "It's all about me, it's all for me, and I'll do whatever it takes to take care of me." The core word is to subtract, which means to withdraw or take away as a part from the whole. Subtracters are uncertain about who they are and what they have to offer, and typically they use their gifts and talents to manipulate, control, and take away from people. Consciously and unconsciously, Subtracters are afraid and intimidated by the gifts and talents that others bring to the world. Subtracters leave your life lacking and fragmented. Little by little your life begins to decrease and fall apart. Why? Because Subtracters work to strip you of your confidence, resources, joy, peace, and self-esteem in a very structured way.

Most Subtracters do not realize how much they subtract from others. I do not believe that some people want to subtract or consciously subtract from others, however, most Subtracters are socialized to use their power negatively at a young age. As a result, they learn to subtract from others as a way of life. In my heart, I know that Subtracters, when caringly confronted, can and will change.

Subtracters can be subtle or blatant. Some Subtracters destroy you little by little until one day you realize that your life is almost empty. You're negative and sad, you question your abilities, and sometimes, you're even financially broke. Subtracters don't really care about who you are, only about what you have that they can take and use for themselves. Their goal is to make themselves feel better by taking away from others. They are often very insecure, sad, and bitter people. Often, they live with unresolved issues that stem from childhood. At their core, Subtracters want to be accepted, to be loved, to feel as though they matter to the world. Instead of striving to be more

Subtracters can be subtle or blatant.

lovable, kind, giving people, Subtracters usually blame others for their problems and go about life decreasing and in some cases, destroying the lives of others. We all have had Subtracters in our lives. When Subtracters show up, our lives usually become more complicated and often harder to live.

Be careful, Subtracters often come in the form of someone who needs your help. Most Subtracters do not intentionally try to take advantage of you. They may not even realize their subtracting behavioral patterns. I once knew a young woman who was constantly subtracting from my life but I didn't understand or realize it. I found myself helping her out of the same messy situations time and time again. Every time I dealt with the young woman, I gave up my time, money, resources, and energy. When I was around this woman, I literally felt my energy being subtracted by her negative perspective and constant cycle of problems. One day, I wondered why she was in my life, what she was offering my life, and how I was helping her. I realized she had become a "Leech." She was sucking every bit of

energy, time, resources, and money out of me. I
needed to let her go. It was one of the hardest
things I've ever had to do but it was necessary. It
was amazing how much that young woman had
subtracted from my life.

Confidence Annihilators

You must understand that eventually,
whether consciously or unconsciously, Subtracters
will strip you of your confidence and annihilate
any goals, dreams, or vision that you have for
your own life. The moment you
begin to think positively about
yourself and your life, a
Subtracter may show up. The
Subtracters nature can be to discourage you from whatever you are trying to
accomplish. They cause you to question your
ability to succeed.

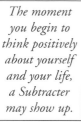

*The moment
you begin to
think positively
about yourself
and your life,
a Subtracter
may show up.*

Subtracters are particularly dangerous because
they sometimes think they are doing you a favor
when they discourage you. Why? Because
Subtracters are afraid to fail and they mostly live
in a world of "I wish I would have, could have,
should have." Subtracters will tell you blatantly

that you can't do something because they tried and it didn't work for them. Subtracters are people whose self-confidence is *stuck* in failure and they don't want anyone around them to succeed because they don't want to be reminded of their own failure.

Some years ago, I noticed a mother and daughter had moved into the house next door. The daughter was a new mother. I also had a young child so I decided to introduce myself and ask the young mom if she wanted to take a walk with the children. She accepted the invitation and said her mother wanted to join us. Our walk ended up being a "Put-Down" session by the mother about her daughter for having a baby, not finishing college, on and on and on. By the end of the walk, my heart was hurting for the young woman. I knew that her mother was a severe Subtracter who would never allow her daughter to develop healthy a confidence and self-esteem. I wanted to tell the daughter, *"Get out, run for your life!"* because I knew that her mother would never value or honor her as a successful and powerful person. The mother's perspective was one of failure and fear.

Unfortunately, most Subtracters think they are helping you when they put you down, talk negatively, or even call you names. They actually think they are doing you a favor. Some will even tell you they are looking out for you and that they are the only person you can really trust. It's a *lie!* If someone is constantly making you doubt your talents, abilities, gifts, and strengths, then you need to stop and listen and decide whether the person is helping or hurting you.

Remember, you have the gift of choice! No one can come and tell you who can be in your life. That's your job. But if a Subtracter is taking away your confidence, then you must make a decision about that person.

Needs-Driven People

Subtracters are often "needy" people who have complex and "messy" lives filled with constant "drama." Subtracters don't want to solve their problems; they simply want to have a story to tell others. Subtracters are great complainers who live in a state of "nothing is going right for me." What is most difficult about Subtracters is figuring out whether they really want help to solve their problems or whether they just like having something to talk about. If someone tells you about a problem every day for a year and does not seek any solutions to the problem, then s(he) really doesn't want to solve the problem. I heard a pastor say once, "Don't complain about what you're willing to permit." In other words, if you're not going to do something about the problem, stop talking about it!

Subtracters not only talk about their needs most of the time, but they also bring those needs into your life. The goal of the Subtracter is to make your life as "messy" and dramatic as theirs. Why? Because Subtracters are not interested in solving the problems or getting rid of the drama; they are only interested in getting more people involved in the "mess" so they can feel wanted and loved. This produces a false sense of belonging and community for the Subtracter.

Think about people you might work with. Is there someone who comes to work every day with a problem? What do they do? They go from person to person talking about their problems and getting others involved. It's a *set up!* Don't go for it. If Subtracters come along with a problem, the one way to stop the conversation is to ask, "What are you going to do about this? How will you solve this problem?" It's time to stop talking about the problem and *do* something about it! Subtracters don't enjoy these kinds of questions or conversation and probably will walk away accusing you of hurting their feelings or offending them.

Gi'me That

Subtracters will not only strip you of your confidence, goals, and dreams; they may also want your resources. Subtracters often want you to give them money, goods, and resources. They know how to ask and manipulate you to feel guilty about them and what they need. Keep in mind, Subtracters often live with needs or wants in their lives so their behavior becomes a cycle of finding ways to fulfill their needs. Many Subtracters only show up in your

> *Subtracters often want you to give them money, goods, and resources.*

life when they need something or are in trouble. Interestingly, when they appear with their needs, they expect you to stop your life and solve their needs.

A person I once knew and thought was a friend turned out to be a Subtracter. As I reflected on our relationship, I realized that she only came around me or called when she needed something. Usually, she needed resources like a place to stay, or a favor done, or a job, or money. It never failed, when she called, I knew my life would be subtracted.

Aren't we supposed to help some people? Absolutely. Remember the law of "seed, time, and harvest?" It's important to sow into the lives of others. In other words, giving to others and helping others is critical to being a powerful person who is positive and influential. Subtracters, however, become a danger to your life because they make a habit of taking your resources and consequently taking advantage of you. The key is that you must come to distinguishbetween someone who is using you and someone who sincerely needs you

> *The key is that you must come to distinguish between someone who is using you and someone who sincerely needs you to be an Adder in his/her life.*

to be an Adder in his/her life.

Expert Manipulators

You need wisdom about people because Subtracters are expert manipulators who know how to use people. What is a manipulator? Someone who artfully manages or controls in a negative way. Subtracters artfully manage and control your emotions, attitude, and resources for their betterment. They know how to use their influence on you in a shrewd, strategic manner for their own profit. Subtracters can disguise themselves as resources for you but then use you for their own profit. Many Subtracters are smart thinkers, but are hurtful people.

I ran across one of the greatest Subtracters of my life when I was a graduate student. This Subtracter was a professor who asked me to help with some research. I was honored and appreciated the opportunity to learn about a new research topic. When we started working together, the Subtracter was very nice, kind, and friendly. We worked very hard together planning the research and talked about co-publishing the results of the research. As time went on, I realized that I was not only doing the work alone but the professor had little time to talk with me, showed no interest in me as a person, and seemed to forget that I existed other than to ask for the work. I ended up not only doing the research project alone but also documenting and analyzing the data and doing the initial reports about the findings. After I finished all of the work, I was proud to hand over the information and was ready to begin writing the articles with the Subtracter. I called the person many times but never received a return call. Some months later, I heard the person had announced her new book to be published in the next year. The book was about the results from the research project that I had done.

This Subtracter had taken a year of my time, resources, energy, and intellect and never once said thank you. It was a hard lesson but I eventually forgave the Subtracter because I did not want bitterness and resentment to fill my heart.

> *Subtracters don't particularly care who you are but they do care about what you can do for them.*

Subtracters don't particularly care who you are but they do care about what you can do for them and how they can manipulate your resources, energy, knowledge, time, and money for their own purposes. They are truly powerful people.

Unfortunately, many of us are taught to be Subtracters; we are taught to manipulate. Even small children learn the art of manipulation. Have you ever seen a small child sitting in the high chair with a toy in his hands? What does s(he) do with the toy? You're right, s(he) drops it on the floor! Then what does s(he) do? S(he) looks at you and even though s(he) can't speak clearly, his/her actions say, "Well, don't just sit there; can't you see I'm helpless here? *Pick it up!*" You read the non-verbal message and pick up the toy. Then what happens? Yes, the child drops it again and gives you that look and so the cycle of manipulation begins. You have some choices. You can make a game of it and pick up the toy a few times and talk baby talk with the child, but then you tell the child it's time to stop and you stop. Or you can allow yourself to be manipulated by that child and find yourself picking up after him for the rest of your *life!* I know some people like that. They are now grown-up children who go around dropping things in life and look for everyone around to pick up the mess! I'm sure you know several people. What is my point? Subtracters know how to manipulate you so be careful.

Subtracters come in every personality type. Some are soft-spoken, seemingly helpless people who operate with a "Oh me, Oh my" perspective on life. Some are quiet, thinking, subtle people who use their mood to manipulate you. You walk around not wanting to upset these people because you never know how they'll respond. Some have extroverted, strong, type-A personalities and tell you straight out, "It's my way or the highway." Some come across as happy, fun people who constantly want you to do something, go somewhere, and spend money. There is no stereotype for Subtracters; they come in all shapes, sizes, colors, and personalities. The one key factor is that **all** Subtracters consistently take things out of your life, seek to control you on some level, and operate from a "what's in it for me" attitude. The bottom line is that Subtracters are powerful people who can cause you great distress and decrease, if you let them.

Time Thieves

A major goal of the Subtracters is to steal your time. Subtracters understand the value of time more than most. They know that if they waste your time by involving you in their messy lives, problems, or personal projects, that you will abandon your real goals and vision for life. One of the main tactics of Subtracters is the telephone. They call and talk to you about absolutely nothing for hours. Their conversation is not interesting, informative, or helpful. Most of the time, Subtracters talk to you about other people. Basically they call and gossip for hours on end. Subtracters will also stop at your house uninvited and just "hang out" for hours at a time. They don't help you cook, clean, get work done, solve problems, *nothing!* They just "hang out" and sometimes even eat up your food! Their hang-out time at your house is another opportunity to tell you their problems, gossip, and put down any goals or aspirations that you might have. People who have constant doses of Subtracters in their

lives will lose self-confidence and become addict-
ed to having "drama" in their lives.

It is important to remember that Subtracters
are time thieves, because at some level, they
understand that time is a valuable and powerful
gift in our lives. Subtracters, especially the "professional" ones, understand that you become your
habits and that how you use your time determines your habits in life.

Some Subtracters don't realize how much of
your time they use. You become a part of their
habits. For example, do you have family members
who have no life, who are going nowhere in life,
only complain about their lives, and come to
your house every other day to just sit and hang
around? Family members do this sometimes
because they understand that they have a "Just Is"
relationship and think that you owe them something. Well, my revelation was that I was not
obligated to have family folk arrive uninvited to
just hang out at my house. If they do come,
they'd better be prepared to work! Help cook,
clean, garden, solve problems, something!

Subtracters like taking away time and you

must learn to manage the influence that these powerful people have in your life or you will become *stuck* in a cycle of mediocrity and hopelessness. Time is a powerful gift, so use it well.

I Want POWER!

Don't be mistaken, Subtracters, whether they know it or not, are very powerful people who exercise their power through influence and control. We all have Subtracters in our lives. The question is how much influence will you allow them to have over you? Rethink who the Subtracters are in your life. What kinds of power do they have? What choices will you have to make about these people? An old saying is that "Knowledge is power;" I disagree with that. The question is, "How does knowledge become power? I think that the exercise or the application of knowledge is what brings power into your life.

Some people realize that some of the most powerful people in their lives are Subtracters. Do you just dismiss those people from your life? Well, if a Subtracter is negative to the point of physical and emotional abuse, then you must make some difficult choices about their role and influence in your life. But what if the Subtracters in your life are subtle takers of your energy, emotions, visions, and dreams? What if your Subtracter is a parent who constantly reminds you that you should not try anything new, learn anything different, meet any new people because you never know what's going to happen? What if you have a long time friend who questions your abilities every time s(he) sees you? What if you are dating a person who constantly puts you down?

Subtracters are so powerful that you must clarify your expectations about how you want to be treated, how you want to communicate, and how you want to interact with them. Otherwise, Subtracters simply choose for you. They make you feel as though it's *ok* to treat you as if you're a nobody, that it's *ok* to take away your energy, that it's *ok* to annihilate your confidence, that it's *ok* to steal your dreams.

The Most Difficult Subtracters

The most influential Subtracters are parents, family members, or close, long-time friends. These people are difficult because so much of our emotions and energy get wrapped up into the relationships. These Subtracters have a way of reminding you of your past faults and mistakes. It's hard to break away from them. For example, I mentored a young woman who lived on the streets of urban Chicago for about three years. I realized that she wouldn't reach her potential because too many family members were Subtracters in her life. I finally told her that if she ever wanted to live a life of power, vision, destiny, and success, she would have to walk away from some of her family members. Delivering this message to the young woman was difficult but I knew that the "Just Is" Subtracters in her life were too powerful. If she wanted to change, she would have to find a new environment and new people, like Adders, to influence her life. Her Subtracters were out to keep her trapped in failure, fear, and poverty.

Now, think about people you listed as powerful in your life. Are any of those people Subtracters? Are you a Subtracter? This work is hard to do because it's "plain old painful" to face our realities, however, we must face our realities if we are to find the powerful person inside of us. We can no longer live in denial. Some of you

> *Some of you will have to tell your Subtracters, "You Gotta Go, I Don't Know Where, But You Have To Get Out Of My Life."*

might have to walk away from your Subtracters until you are strong enough to deal with them. Some of you may have to confront your Subtracters and give them new expectations for how you want to be treated. Some of you will have to tell your Subtracters, "You Gotta Go, I Don't Know Where, But You Have To Get Out Of My Life." This is very hard to do but it may be necessary to save *your life!*

Some of you might choose to learn to manage your Subtracters and teach them how to add to your life. As noted, some Subtracters who hurt people are crying out for help and they only know how to take from others. You must choose a path for dealing with Subtracters; no one else can tell you which path to take. This will require your honesty and personal leadership. You must now lead yourself and make healthy, positive choices for your life.

Let me warn you that some Subtracters won't

leave without a fight. They know how to fight, how to use their power to control you, and how to manipulate you. So think hard. If you believe in prayer, pray. Ask God to show you how to handle Subtracters.

I had to confront a major "Just Is" Subtracter in my life. It was one of the most difficult things I've ever done. I was frightened of this person and did not know how to tell them that I could no longer allow them in my life and that they were single handedly ruining my life. After many years (yes, years!) and much prayer, I found the courage, energy, and personal leadership to confront them about how they treated me and to tell them they could no longer be in my life. It was a horrible day. But the following days, weeks, years have been phenomenal. I have grown tremendously and have found potential, gifts, and talents in me that I never knew existed when I was trapped by the opinions and influence of that Subtracter.

We all have our own life battles. The key is that you must take action and lead yourself so that you

> *We all have our own life battles. The key is that you must take action and lead yourself*

Where do you start? By being honest about who the Subtracters are and understanding what they are taking from you.

become the powerful person you were created to be. Where do you start? By being honest about who the Subtracters are and understanding what they are taking from you and how they are influencing your thoughts, actions, emotions, and dreams.

Spotting a Subtracter

How do you spot a Subtracter? Well, you can tell a Subtracter by what they take out of your life. When a Subtracter is operating, you might:

- Doubt your abilities, goals, and vision;
- Second-guess your decisions and actions;
- Dislike who you are;
- Lose confidence in who you are and what you can do;
- Find your our life becomes cluttered with "drama" and "messy" situations;
- Notice you're spending more money on the Subtracter;
- Notice you don't have time to do what you find important;
- Lose your sense of humor, your joy;

- Become fearful about learning new information
- Begin to complain about your life and develop a Subtracter complex.

Take a moment and review your Influential People list. Do you have any Subtracters on that list? What actions will you take to deal with your Subtracters? If you know what you are going to do, take a moment to write down how this will be accomplished.

Who Are Your Subtracters?

_____

_____

_____

_____

_____

_____

What Actions will I take to deal with my subtracters?

∞ _____

_____

∞ _____

_____

∞ _____

_____

Are You A Subtracter?

If you've read this chapter and realize that you are a Subtracter, then you must choose to change. You can change! Be honest with yourself. Begin today to learn to add, not subtract from others. You will find that your life will become peaceful, fulfilling, and purposeful. You will begin to give to others and in return, your life will blossom with people and resources. You will also begin to appreciate who you are and what you have to offer others. You do not have to be a

> *You do not have to be a Subtracter for life. You can change!*

Subtracter for life. You can change!

Becoming an Adder

The journey to becoming an Adder begins with your honesty. Think about how you treat people, talk to people, and interact with people. Now, what do you like or dislike about who you are? *Be honest!* Evaluate yourself, your actions and the people in your life. Ask yourself hard questions like: "Why do I treat people the way that I do?, Why do I subtract others?, Why is everything always about me?, Why do I need to control and manipulate others?" Now, begin changing your attitude about yourself, people and life. Begin developing new behavior patterns towards others. Instead of constantly thinking about yourself and your needs, start thinking about others. Instead of trying to get from others, start giving to others with no strings attached. Begin to use your energy to help others, not to hurt them. Start thinking about what other people might need and begin adding to them without expecting anything in return. Start complimenting others on their gifts, talents and abilities instead of being intimidated.

Chapter 8

THE DIVIDERS IN YOUR LIFE

Have you ever met " tricky" people? People you just can't seem to figure out? People who for no apparent reason really want to be your friend, to be an important part of your life? People who want to become your "best friend" over night? At first, these people are extra kind, understanding, and gracious to you. They often show an unnatural passion for wanting to be around you and immediately begin to take up space in your life.

At first, you may be amazed that s(he) has taken such interest in you. Then as time passes, s(he) becomes demanding. S(he) begins to be around you all of the time, s(he) may get upset if you want to be with other people who care about you, and s(he) may begin to dictate how and who you spend your time with. Before you know what is going on, s(he) has not only taken up your time and energy but s(he) has moved into your life. You find yourself leaving your faithful friends behind. You no longer see your family members who care about you. You find yourself declining invitations from colleagues. What has happened to your life? You just came in contact with the third type of powerful people who will influence your life, the Divider.

Dividers are notorious for great starts in building relationships, platonic or romantic. They are tricky because they appear, at first, to want the best for you. Then they change. Unfortunately, by the time most people realize that they are dealing with a Divider, they have given up so much of who they really are that disconnecting becomes very difficult. As we will discuss later in this chapter, disconnecting from a Divider can be very painful and even dangerous.

Who Are Dividers?

Of the four powerful people you will meet in your life, Dividers are the most manipulative, deceptive, and dangerous. Why? Because Dividers ultimately want to have full control over your life. Control is very important to a Divider because it is their source of power over people. Dividers know that if you consciously or unconsciously give them control over your life, they will automatically have power over you, your goals, your vision, and your destiny.

What does the base word of Divider mean? It means to separate, disconnect, and reduce your personal power through diversion and distraction. The old slogan of "divide and conquer" is the theme of a Divider's way of life.

The Divider's mission is to dismantle your goals, visions, and dreams through distraction and false purpose. Dividers don't care about where you want to go; Dividers mostly care about how to manipulate you into achieving their personal agenda.

Their mission is to distract you from your "real purpose" in life. Have you ever found yourself thinking, "What am I doing? Why am I working with this person? Why am I in this situation? Who is controlling my life?" These are all "alert" questions, red flags to motivate you to really examine who you are, what you are doing, and who is in your life.

Dividers are very insecure people who need to prey on others to make themselves feel good. They may need your talent to make them look good. They may need your friendship to promote their need for acceptance, control, and power. Dividers often need others to be their energy and power source. Dividers are also extremely possessive people who exhibit their insecurity by making you feel guilty about not being with them. Dividers have an entitlement mentality. They believe they are entitled to be the center of your life, to control your life, and to dictate who you are and what you do.

Dividers are intimidated by competence and are often very competitive. They have difficulty dealing with others who are better than them. When you become excellent, they begin to see you as a threat. Dividers are great manipulators of important information and facts. They use information to keep your trust, while keeping you away from the total truth about them. They tend to be two-faced, using information you've given them to maintain control over you.

> *Dividers work very hard to keep you from knowing the "full" story about their motives, agenda, and behavior.*

Dividers work very hard to keep you from knowing the "full" story about their motives, agenda, and behavior.

Both Subtracters and Dividers will negatively influence your life. The difference, however, is that Subtracters are not always conscious of how they are influencing your life. Subtracters are also mostly thinking about how to fulfill their own needs by using your gifts, talents and abilities. For the most part, they want just their needs met. Dividers, on the other hand, are motivated by a need to control your life. ***Whereas a subtracter might leave you empty and lacking, a Divider could destroy your life.*** Dividers are much more strategic about using their personal power to control your thoughts, actions and ultimately, your life. This is the danger of Dividers.

A Divider Story

When I was in college, I encountered a Divider in the form of a boyfriend. At first, this person was overly kind and understanding and giving. He gave me candy, flowers, and nice notes. He walked with me to my classes and took me on nice dates. I was enamored by his level of attention and found it very refreshing and exciting. As I got to know him, I began to notice he always wanted to be around me. He began to have an "attitude" if I hung out with my other friends, mostly women. It became clear that he wanted me to have only one relationship and that was with him. He wanted to be the center of my life. He began to talk down my friends, to discourage my passion for education, and take up more of my time. He also began to play guilt games with me when I had to study or wanted to spend time with my other friends. Every time I looked around, he was there. I began feeling claustrophobic in the relationship and developed a guilt complex about not wanting to "hurt" or "disappoint" him because after all, he had been so "nice" to me. But instinctively, I knew something was wrong. He started talking about getting married and quitting school, a plan contrary to my purpose of getting an education, then having a career, then marriage and a family. He began manipulating me and trying to divide me from my purpose in college by challenging me with: "If I really loved him," I would let him control my life. I was young, only about 19, and I was vulnerable. I soon began to lose my friends who cared about me because this Divider was chasing them away. Somehow, by the grace of God, I knew that his tactics, motives, and behaviors were wrong. No one had ever taught me about Dividers or the power of people, but I knew that I was dealing with a powerful person, who was trying to control my life. Deep in my heart, I knew he would ultimately divide me, separate me, and distract me from my life purpose and destiny. It took every ounce of courage that I had to tell him that I would no longer date him, see him, or hang out with him. I had to separate myself from him. What I wasn't prepared for was that he would retaliate with more guilt trips that eventually turned into publicly blaming me for causing him to fail his classes and quit school. Eventually, he did fail his courses and quit college.

This experience taught me some painful lessons about the power of people. I learned to watch more carefully how people entered my life and to examine their motives for wanting to be in my life. It took time to rebuild the true friendships that the Divider had nearly destroyed. One of the lessons is that ***time will always reveal a divider***. Why? Because Dividers usually enter your life looking like a passionate Adder or Multiplier, but in time, their true motives for control and power over your life become very clear. Remember, ***time*** has a way of revealing authentic character, core behaviors, and driving motives.

> *I learned to watch more carefully how people entered my life and to examine their motives for wanting to be in my life.*

> *Remember, time has a way of revealing authentic character, core behaviors, and driving motives.*

Divider Dagger #1

What daggers do Dividers use to separate you from your purpose, vision, and life goals? First, they work overtime to keep you away from the Adders and Multipliers in your life. They see Adders and Multipliers as enemies to their overall agenda of separating you from powerful people who want you to achieve your personal best. Dividers know that people who genuinely care about your destiny will challenge you to change, examine your people connections, and pursue your life purpose. A Divider wants you to be committed to his/her agenda, not your own.

Dividers also know that Adders and Multipliers will help you take a "reality" check of your life; they challenge you to ask yourself criti-

> *The more you know yourself, the more powerful you become.*

cal questions about your relationships and goals. People who think clearly and assess their lives accurately intimidate Dividers because the essence of critically thinking about oneself leads to personal empowerment. The more you know yourself, the more powerful you become.

Recently, I was invited by a respected colleague to a "release" party. I'd never been to a "release" party and thought that I was being invited to witness the unveiling of a new product line, music endeavor, or book. This person had recently married a prominent businessman and lived in an small mansion in an upscale section of the city. When I visited their home, I witnessed what appeared to be an unusually romantic and inspiring marriage relationship.

As I entered the house for this "release" party, I felt a strangeness and immediately knew something was wrong. Others, who had arrived before me, sat around in small clusters talking and laughing. On the surface, it looked like a typical party, but something was different about this group. They were all women from diverse ethnic groups and social statuses.

As I walked in to greet the group, my colleague pulled me aside to tell me she was divorcing her husband. She explained that he had decided to end the marriage and that she had been betrayed. In public, she explained, he was gracious and romantic, but in private, he was controlling and cold. She described his amazing entrance into her life, sweeping her off her feet, promising her a wonderful life of love, intrigue, travel, and spirituality. Shortly after marriage, she began to notice the element of control he wanted over her life. He systematically detached her from her Adders and Multipliers by talking them down or making her feel guilty for wanting them in her life. He was determined to be the only person in her life.

One of her most vivid examples, was how her new husband refused to let her sister visit their new, beautiful home. He knew that her sister was a mentor and true friend and he was intimidated by their relationship. The woman finally saw the real person she had married. When she began to challenge these controlling and manipulative behaviors, her husband moved out all of the beautiful things he had bought for the house and left.

The "release" party was her way of recreating her network of Adders and Multiplier, women who would help her bear the burden of losing what appeared to be a perfect life and restarting her real life again. It was one of the most interesting events I have ever attended. My heart went out to her because she had been trapped by a Divider, who threatened to insulate, isolate, and control her life. Her only hope was to reach out to her Adders and Multipliers who would help her think critically about life so that she could regain her sense of personal power. This woman is very savvy, highly educated, and very connected in the community. Anyone can be trapped by a Divider.

Divider Dagger #2

A Divider's goal is to get you to trust only him/her, believe only him/her, want only him/her in your life. Why is this dangerous? Because it gives Dividers power and control over your emotions and your ability to think critically. Eroding your trust for others is a key mission of Dividers. The logic is simple: If you don't trust yourself or anyone else in your life, then you must depend on Dividers for advice, mentoring, and counsel. Dividers use your dependence on them to establish more control of your life. Don't underestimate the thinking power of a Divider; remember, they are expert manipulators.

> *A Divider's goal is to get you to trust only him/her, believe only him/her, want only him/her in your life.*

What tactics do Dividers use to lure you away from trusting others? The major tactic is lying to you about people who genuinely care for you. Dividers often attack their character and provide you with false information or misinformation to make you doubt them. Before you know it, you begin to believe the picture the

Divider paints. This often leads to misunderstanding, miscommunication, and ultimately the demise of your trust in others and your relationships with others.

One of the most powerful schemes that a Divider uses is to manipulate you into thinking s(he) is really the *only* person who "truly" cares about you and s(he) has your best interest in mind. At this point, a Divider can begin to really control your life because s(he) would have successfully isolated you from others who genuinely care about you.

I am an avid fan of professional football and I believe that the fall season was made for fellowship at church, football, food … and Sunday afternoon naps! In the fall of 2000, a popular television network advertised a new show during the football games called "Temptation Island." I was appalled by the concept of seeking to tempt others sexually with no honor for morality, integrity, or sexual ethics. I was indignant that the network would throw what I consider "emotional, and immoral trash" into my home during a football game. The first time the advertisement was aired I was shocked, then I moved from that emotion to disgust, then to social activism. I began telling people that we needed to do something about this show. Why? Because the core message that "Temptation Island" espoused was that you can't trust anyone, that you can't really love anyone, that love's only value is sexual, and that lying to get your way sexually is a way of life. These sorts of shows systematically teach viewers how to be dangerous Dividers. They teach society how to use people, how to lie, and how to use sexual power to destroy others and themselves. More than ever before, our youth in this country need to know without a doubt that "love is real and unconditional." "Temptation Island" and shows like it clearly illustrate Dividers' power. Interestingly. that show was canceled shortly after.

Divider Dagger #3

A Divider wants you to give him/her your time, your energy, and your attention. He wants to be the center of your world. He wants to create your world and get the credit for making you into somebody. Remember, these are insecure people who need you to boost their self-esteem.

Many Dividers suffer from a gut level need for unconditional love. As children, they often didn't get love, support, and care from their parents. Therefore, they create ways to manipulate people into loving them, looking up to them, and thinking they are the greatest. Dividers must be the center of attention. If they play a sport, a Divider might be the one who never passes the ball; they're "ball hogs!!" My seven year-old son plays soccer, and one day, I commented about the extraordinary skills of one of his teammates. The teammate was the shortest player on the team and had what seemed to be a natural gift of maneuvering the ball and knowing how to score points. To my surprise, my son exclaimed with disgust in his voice, "But mom, he never passes the ball!" I was surprised by his reaction and had nothing to say but "Oh!" At the next soccer game, I watched this teammate and his approach to the game. Sure enough, (or some would say "Sho Nuf!") every time he had the ball, he kept it to himself until he either scored or kicked it out of bounds. His teammates would yell at him, get into position for a pass or wave at him, but to no avail. He was going to be the main player, the center of attention, and that was it.

Dividers go to drastic means to be the center of attention in your life. They often begin a relationship by giving you unconditional attention, flattery, gifts, and promises. But sooner or later, they demand that they share you with no one, including those on your relationship team (parents, good friends, trusted mentors, and colleagues) who are waving and yelling at the Divider to share you.

Who Are the Dividers In Your Life?

What Are They Doing To Divide You?

∽ _____

_____

∽ _____

_____

∽ _____

_____

Demoting Dividers

How do you deal with or confront a Divider
in your life? Many times, people who finally
understand Dividers often have become attached
emotionally, spiritually, and sometimes economi-
cally. Demoting a Divider requires clear action
on your part. You must call a Divider for who
s(he) is, a Divider. This might be painful and difficult but you must _be honest_!

∽ Begin to seek the people who have been
chased out of your life and begin
rebuilding relationships with them. This
will give you new perspective, new

strength, and the support needed to confront the Divider.

∽ Search for your Adders and Multipliers, who will support you and help you build your courage to confront the Dividers.

∽ Make a decision to confront the Divider. If you believe in prayer, I recommend asking God for wisdom to know when and where to confront the Divider. Remember Dividers are dangerous; they are very possessive. They will not just let you go or share you with others because they would have to give up control over you. The last thing a Divider wants is for you to think for yourself!

> *The last thing a Divider wants is for you to think for yourself!*

∽ Find the courage to confront the person in a loving and gentle way. Keep in mind that many Dividers just want to be loved.

∽ Be ready for a "Divider Explosion" or a "Divider Denial." A Divider could explode emotionally and cause you physical harm or a Divider can cut you off, deny your existence, and/or treat you as an enemy. You have no control over either reaction. You are only responsible for your own reaction. I believe that if you confront him/her in a loving, kind way that you can walk away in peace knowing you did the right thing. Sometimes, a Divider will listen to you even though it might really hurt him/her, face the realities of who s(he) is, and decide to change his/her ways. S(he) might decide to use his/her personal power for good and not for destruction. It can happen! Caution, be wise. Only you will know exactly how to handle the Dividers in your life. Plan for your own safety - avoid being alone and isolated with them.

∞ Be ready to start your life again. Often, a person who escapes an extreme Divider has to rebuild the emotional and spiritual fabric of his/her life. You have to rediscover who you really are, what

> *Be ready to start your life again.*

83

you really want, and who are the important Adders and Multipliers in your life. This might be painful but, in time, you will be thankful you decided to demote your Dividers.

> *In time, you will be thankful you decided to demote your Dividers.*

What Action Steps Will You Take To Demote Your Dividers? Be Specific!

∞ _____

_____

∞ _____

_____

∞ _____

_____

Are You A Divider?

What can you do if after reading this chapter, you have honestly concluded that you are a Divider? Be honest and ask yourself some critical questions: Why am I a Divider? Why did I become this way? What do I really want in life? Where can I get help in talking about these issues? Are there any Adders or Multipliers in my life? If you believe in prayer, ask God to forgive you for the harm you have caused others. Then, forgive yourself and ask people you have hurt for forgiveness.

At first, people who don't understand you have been a Divider will think you are a little crazy! That's *ok*; it's *ok* to be called crazy for doing the *right* thing. Decide to change, to give up the power you have over others and learn to honor and value the gifts, talents, and abilities of others. Step down from your position as the center of life and accept that some people have greater needs than yours.

My pastor once said that people are so complex they need a whole network of people to understand and work with them. No one person can be everything to you. This is a hard lesson for Dividers but it is possible to change. You will have to humble yourself and begin honoring

> *No one person can be everything to you.*

greatness in others. Remember that mathematically, division is in the same family with multiplication. If you have Divider traits, then you probably have Multiplier traits as well. Choose to be a Multiplier instead. *Yes, you can choose. That's why you are powerful!*

Chapter 9

THE GREAT MULTIPLIER

Miraculous Mentors

I've waited for what seems like years to write about Multipliers. Why? Because of all the powerful people in this world, Multipliers are probably the most powerful and most influential. Multipliers are miraculous.

If you are experiencing any kind of "ceiling" in your life — financial, professional, spiritual, emotional, social, or intellectual — begin looking for, even praying for, a Multiplier. A ceiling is when you can visualize yourself doing something new but don't know how to start. In a way, it's as if you have gone to the end of yourself.

We hear about the "glass ceiling" in the business world, especially as it relates to women and people of color. I recently attended a party for a colleague at a home that had a glass ceiling built into it. Until then, the term "glass ceiling" never really made sense to me. But, when I began to look through that literal glass ceiling, I understood about seeing but not actually touching or experiencing the artifacts on the other side of the glass. I was given a view but no access or opportunity. When you can see yourself discovering, understanding, and using your personal power but you have no access or specific opportunity beyond your "ceiling," then you must search for a Multiplier.

The word Multiplier has two root words, multi and ply. Multi means many, more than one, or abundant. Ply means thickness, layer, and to carry on. When connected, these words become quite powerful! Multiply means to increase, double, add to, boost, enlarge, expand, magnify, and amplify. Isn't that exciting? I don't know about you but those words make me want to *shout for joy!* Why? Because, there are people in or around your life who can literally help to enlarge, magnify, amplify, expand, and increase you!

Here's the secret. Most Multipliers find great

joy in helping others but they don't go around announcing that they are Multipliers. As a matter of fact, when someone is quick to want to help me, I often question his/her motives. Does s(he) want to help me because s(he) needs something from me or needs to be in control or needs someone to think s(he) is great? False multipliers seek weak, needy people and offer to "help" them. These connections often prove to be destructive and negative encounters.

Real Multipliers are usually very caring, sincere people who have a gift for discovering people with potential and a sense of purpose. Multipliers are observant people who watch you for years before offering to be of assistance. Many times, Multipliers will wait until you ask them for help, advice, or counsel. Multipliers are also good listeners. They understand that "It's not about me." Their satisfaction comes from seeing your success.

Here's another secret: Multipliers already know who they are and they really don't need you. Why is this important? Because Multipliers aren't

> *Multipliers already know who they are and they really don't need you.*

looking for a "payback;" they don't have a secret web waiting to get you entangled. They don't have strings attached; their genuine joy is to see you succeed. That's it! Personally, I like Multipliers because they are so confident in who they are that they are not easily intimidated or offended by anything I do or say. They have learned the great life principle of not taking things personally.[5]

Multipliers also know how to deliver a "hard" word when needed. A motivating factor for Multipliers is to help you be your most excellent and powerful self. That's it!

> *A motivating factor for Multipliers is to help you be your most excellent and powerful self.*

I have had phenomenal Multipliers in my life, people who I will forever thank God for. These people looked beyond my young undisciplined passion for life and saw my potential to significantly touch the lives of people all over the world.

I have had to endure harsh words from Multipliers. I have had my feelings hurt by Multipliers but I have come to understand that because Multipliers are so powerful, you only get a few of them, so don't miss the opportunity. Begin thinking about who your Multipliers are. Look at your list of influential powerful people. Are any of them Multipliers? Later, we will discuss how to find Multipliers, but first, you must understand and eliminate common myths associated with Multipliers.

Multiplier Myths

Many people mistake Multiplier relationships for friendships. I must warn you that Multipliers aren't necessarily your buddy or friend. Sometimes, you may feel that Multipliers don't even like you because they aren't necessarily concerned about making you feel good about yourself.

Sometimes, Multipliers appear to get into your business or even embarrass you. Multipliers have difficulty operating in your life if you are easily offended or easily hurt. Recently, I had an incident with a young woman who sought me as a Multiplier for her life. The young woman was about to make a public professional mistake and I had to confront her publicly about her choices. My comment to her was not nice or diplomatic;

in fact, it was direct, to the point, and somewhat harsh. My intention was not to hurt her but to make her think quickly about her actions. Later when we talked privately, she thanked me but it was a painful experience for both of us. Don't make a habit of confronting people publicly, but as a Multiplier, you may occasionally need to publically confront them to keep them from making a potentially bad choice. Multipliers can be severely honest with you so be prepared to "suffer" through what may seem like harsh or sometimes difficult questions and comments.

Multipliers aren't necessarily attracted only to smart, competent people who know how to network. The truth is that Multipliers are not attracted to people who think they "know it all" or have an "I've made it" attitude. As a matter of fact, Multipliers tend to stay away from people who seem to have an answer or argument for everything or people who constantly talk about themselves. Why? Simple: If you know it all, then you have nothing to learn,

> *Multipliers tend to stay away from people who seem to have an answer or argument for everything or people who constantly talk about themselves.*

you are unwilling to listen to others, you are unwilling to honor the achievements of others, you are unwilling to humble yourself, and therefore, you cannot be coached or mentored. Multipliers are natural coaches and mentors. They want you to be your best but you must be willing to listen, learn, and work as a team. This is critical because Multipliers realize that unless you are teachable and coachable, you will never gain new knowledge and therefore, never be able to seize new opportunities.

Multipliers don't necessarily have high-level positions with lots of power and money. This is probably the greatest myth. The fact is that a Multiplier can be anyone: a boss, a parent, a colleague, a neighbor,

> *Multipliers don't necessarily have high-level positions with lots of power and money.*

the president of your company, or your children. Multipliers don't have to be in high positions of influence, have lots of money, or be popular.

Sometimes people miss Multipliers because they are busy looking for the "up in front" person to multiply them. The person "up in front" may not multiply you but maybe the person in the cubicle next to you will. How often do we listen to others, study how they talk to and treat us? Is there someone in your life who consistently asks about your goals and your future and encourages you to be successful? Is there someone in your life who is consistently offering to connect you with other people who might share your life goals and interest? Has your boss been trying to help you improve your skills and abilities by giving you constructive feedback? Do you have these people in you life?

We all should have at least three of these people who think we are *awesome!* Someone who believes in you and is your natural cheerleader. Never underestimate the potential of people to be

> *Multipliers are attracted to potential, not position.*

Multipliers in your life. Our society has tricked us into believing that we are only as important as the amount of stuff we accumulate. That's a lie!! Every person is powerful so be on the look out for who can and will multiply your life. Multipliers are attracted to potential, not position.

Multipliers aren't in your life forever. Authentic Multipliers will come and go. They operate in seasons. They may only be called to you for a season and you must be prepared to let them go. Multipliers often operate on a "just on time" basis. The problem occurs when people want to hang on to a Multiplier whose season has passed. Remember, Multipliers are called to move you to another level. Once you get to that level, that Multiplier is no longer needed in that capacity. Multipliers tend to understand this phenomenon but the people they coach, mentor, or lead often do not. Recently, I released one of my great Multipliers. I have had to watch him move on to Multiply others. This person has enlarged, expanded, and increased my life dramatically and I truthfully didn't want to let him go! He did not have problems letting me go; as a matter of fact, he was proud to "release" me.

Multipliers aren't natural givers to everyone. Multipliers are giving and resourceful, but not to everyone. A Multiplier may not be called to you, so don't get jealous of someone else's Multiplier. This is difficult especially when you know Multipliers who are public figures

> *A Multiplier may not be called to you, so, don't get jealous of someone else's Multiplier.*

like pastors, professors, politicians, famous personalities, bosses, for example. I never thought that I would struggle with this feeling. But I had to repent because I was slightly jealous of how my pastor was called to mentor, coach, and personally lead a few people in the church and not others, like *me!* Yes, I did get a little "attitude" but I quickly **got over it!** Why? Because, Multipliers are **called** to you, divinely **connected** to you and uniquely **designed** for you. I have since realized that my pastor was not the Multiplier I needed. You and your Multipliers will understand your divine connection. When that connection is made, your Multipliers will do everything possible to make resources and opportunities available to you. In short, avoid Multiplier jealousy.

Multiplier Types

You will meet two types of Multipliers in your lifetime. Both types are important but their roles and level of impact may differ. Knowing the difference will keep you from missing opportunities and being frustrated with potential Multipliers. The two types are Escalator

Multipliers and Elevator Multipliers. I discovered this idea of escalators and elevators while talking with one of my personal Multipliers about how to help a person get back into college and have a successful life. My Multiplier noted that our job should be to put people on the escalators of life and help them move up to another floor. Then, when that person begins to accumulate successes by reaching new floor levels and gets a clearer vision about life, we should put them on the elevator and punch a floor number that is much higher so they can reach their full potential. This was a powerful visual image for me because in my lifetime, I had witnessed both types of Multipliers.

Escalator Multipliers

Why do Escalator Multipliers come into your life? There are many reasons:

- They want to help you sort out who you are, what you have to offer your society, and what you are all about.
- They can see your potential and feel called to multiply your life.
- They help you build, gain, or realize

confidence in your "climbing" ability. Their goal is to help you understand your personal power and to begin to learn how to use it.

- ☙ They want to teach you how to use opportunities in your life to climb to new levels without using up or destroying those around you.

- ☙ They test your willingness to work hard even when no one sees you. They want to know that you are not using them to seek the front stage.

- ☙ They want to see whether you are for *real*. They don't want or need a name-dropper but someone who genuinely wants to discover his/her personal power so s(he) can help someone else. They work with you to confront any issues of low self-esteem, fear of success, pride, or greed. Escalator Multipliers can easily point out people who only want to be around them for "show" purposes so that they can drop an impressive name at the next event. I witnessed a young woman trying to connect herself to an Escalator Multiplier at a conference. The Escalator Multiplier happened to be an influential woman in her late 40s who helped organize and plan the conference. It was obvious the young woman only wanted to be able to drop the conference organizer's name but had no interest in confronting her own issues of pride and need for the spot light. The Escalator Multiplier was kind to her but clearly was not interested in putting the young woman on an escalator.

∞ They provide opportunities to test your willingness to work hard, listen intently, and reach for new levels.

Escalator Multipliers are critical to realizing personal power. Why? Because, Escalator Multipliers are concerned mostly about motivat-

> *Escalator Multipliers are concerned mostly about motivating you to build your character so that you can manage your own personal power.*

ing you to build your character so that you can manage your own personal power. That's why Escalator Multipliers only take you one step at a time. In time you will reach the new level, but in the process, you will learn how to think critically about who you are, why you are, and your purpose in life. In time, you will learn how to use your power to enhance yourself and others. How? Escalator Multipliers continually challenge you with questions about your life. They are known to interrogate you about your life goals, vision, plans, actions, and attitudes. They require that you think constantly about who you are, why you are, and how you can positively impact society with your personal power.

For example, during a mentoring conversation with a colleague, it was clear to me that she did not realize her personal power. She was stuck at a professional level and she didn't know what to do about it. Having observed her work for almost three years, I was led to ask her a number of hard questions. I asked her:

- what she was passionate about in life,
- what she liked about her job,
- if given the opportunity what kind of job would she like,
- what had kept her in her current position for so long,

- what her vision was,
- whether she had written her vision,
- what her purpose was in life,
- what difference did she want to make in society, and so on.

My tone was very serious because I saw that this young woman was loaded with potential and personal power but she didn't know it. She needed a major mind and spirit jolt to get her on the first step of the escalator. I felt as if I had to push her onto the step! Months later, she admitted that our conversation left her thinking so hard about her life that she even lost her appetite to eat and need to sleep. She had been challenged to think, to discover, and to risk leaving her comfort zone. Many people, myself included, try to avoid Escalator Multipliers because they demand that we do some hard work. You may not always enjoy Escalator Multipliers, but in time, you will learn to cherish and appreciate these people.

The key to Escalator Multipliers is to recognize quickly who they are. Typically, they are interested in your goals, future, and success. You will find that they consistently encourage and compliment you on work well done. They might invite you to work on a committee, task force, or project with them. Sometimes they recommend you for a project or introduce you to others who have similar aspirations.

Here's a clue that will help you keep Escalator Multipliers in your life: When your Escalator Multiplier recommends you for a project, accept the project and do the best job possible! Don't mess up! Why? Because a recommendation means that your Escalator Multiplier has put him/herself on the line for you. This means that you no longer just represent yourself; instead, you now become synonymous with your Escalator Multiplier. This is serious! Many, many people lose their Escalator Multipliers because they fail to produce and be effective when given an opportunity to get on the escalator and climb.

Not long ago, I heard a story about an Escalator Multiplier who had put an aspiring young designer on the escalator by connecting him with a well-known local designer. The local designer agreed to provide the young man with an internship because of his Escalator Multiplier.

As it turned out, the young man didn't understand the process and proceeded to be unpro-
ductive and irresponsible with his internship. The
local designer called the Escalator Multiplier to
share his concerns about the young man's
progress. The Escalator Multiplier's response was
simple and quick, *fire him!* That was it. The
young man made two grave errors: first, he
missed a great opportunity to learn from and be
mentored by one of the best designers in town;
second and more serious, he had damaged a critical relationship with his Escalator Multiplier.
Unfortunately, the young man had failed to see
this escalator opportunity as a way to help him
discover his personal power. The result was that
the Escalator Multiplier could no longer trust
him to work hard and had to end the relationship.

Who are the Escalator Multipliers in your
life? Who are the people asking you hard questions, encouraging you, providing you with new
opportunities for success, and helping you discover your personal power? Take a moment and
write the names of those people and a brief

description about how they have put you on the escalators of life. Remember, Escalator Multipliers can be anyone. They don't have to be the obvious people who are "in charge," "up front," "title carriers," or "popular."

My Escalator Multipliers Are:

∞ _____

_____

∞ _____

_____

∞ _____

_____

Ways They Put Me On An Escalator:

∞ _____

_____

∞ _____

_____

Elevator Multipliers

The second type of multiplier is called an Elevator Multiplier. These multipliers are exciting to have in your life. When you finally get blessed with an Elevator Multiplier, you will know it! How? Because you will begin to reach levels of achievement and personal power that you might never have dreamed possible. Elevator Multipliers only ask you one question: How high do you want to go? If you know, they will find whatever resources you need to get you on the elevator; then they will push the button to the top floor.

Elevator Multipliers usually have access to the positional power, resources, and people needed to propel you. I remember the day one of my Elevator Multipliers asked me what I wanted to do with my talents, skills, abilities, and passion. Thank God, I had taken some time at age 21 to write down what I wanted in life, where I wanted to go, and how I wanted to help my world. No one taught me how to do this. I was fresh out of college and I needed direction. I had always known that I wanted to be a teacher but not in a typical classroom. I wanted to teach the world but I had no idea how I could or would do this. I did know, however, that I needed a doctoral degree in education. I was broke and didn't know anyone who had money, except God! So I wrote down my vision.

Six years later, my Elevator Multiplier asked me, having observed my work with his organization for years, what I wanted to do? I was ready with my answer. I had digested my vision. I knew what I wanted to do. His immediate response was, "you will need a doctoral degree, a Ph.D., to work at that level." Then he proceeded to tell me that he would talk with a professor at the local University who had similar interests and might need a graduate assistant. I didn't understand his multiplier influence until I met with the professor and she invited me to study with her as a graduate student. Being a graduate assistant meant doing research, learning more about education, getting focused about my vision, and most importantly having my education paid for.

My Elevator Multiplier put me on the elevator and pushed the button to the top floor. Years later, he continued to create new opportunities for me so I could discover personal power and experience success.

What if I hadn't been ready to answer the question posed by my Elevator Multiplier? I believe that I would not have a Ph.D. in education or I would be paying off a giant student loan. Why do I say this? You have to be ready to meet the challenge of getting on the elevator. The Elevator Multiplier can't prepare you; that's not the role of the Escalator Multiplier. You have to be prepared to go to the top level.

> *You have to be ready to meet the challenge of getting on the elevator.*

Warning: If you get on that elevator and you are *not* ready, you will suffer greatly and few Elevator Multipliers will come through your life! Once you get on the elevator, you'd better make up your mind to reach deep inside yourself and access your personal power to succeed. Why? The level of influence that Elevator Multipliers have in your life will take you to the top or destroy you. You cannot *fake it* with Elevator Multipliers.

You are either ready to experience that level of influence or you are not!

Who are Elevator Multipliers? How do you know when you have an Elevator Multiplier?

> *You cannot fake it with Elevator Multipliers. You are either ready to experience that level of influence or you are not!*

- They tend to be in positions of power and influence.
- They are usually at the personal level of power that you aspire to.
- They are well connected, networked, and respected in their circle of influence. That is, they know other influential people and they are known to be influential. Remember that Elevator Multipliers are rare and you will be blessed if you have more than one in your lifetime.
- They only mentor people who are passionate and prepared to achieve high levels of personal power. ***They want to be confident that you can't just handle the top floor but manage it gracefully and humbly.***
- They are willing to take a big risk by

loaning out their name and reputation on your behalf.

∞ They have vision to see you beyond yourself. They can see you in the future but require you to be willing to take a leap of faith to achieve that future.

∞ They refuse to accept excuses for failure. They don't believe in failure but only in lessons for life. They require you to work harder, think harder, and create more than other people. They expect you to succeed and to be powerful.

I remember being recommended for a top marketing management job by one of my Elevator Multipliers. I had no idea whether I could do the job, but I trusted my Elevator Multiplier and knew that she would not let me fail. I knew that she believed in me and I was determined not to let her down. The truth was that I had never done this type of job. Nevertheless, she took me off my escalator job, put me on the elevator, and challenged me to a new level of thinking, confidence, and personal power. Not only did I succeed in the job but I learned the great lesson of taking the risk to let others see me beyond myself.

Think about it. Do you have people around you who have consistently challenged you to take a new position, go back to school, or learn a new skill? Have these people promised to support you, network with you, and provide you with resources to get you to that new level in your life? What are you waiting for? Remember, you will experience few Elevator Multipliers in you lifetime, so be prepared. Don't miss the opportunity!

If you know a person who is in a position of power and influence and shows interest in your life's vision, don't be shy! Tell him/her your vision! You don't have to tell him/her every detail, just the basics. For example, I want to positively impact how education takes place for urban youth. That's basic but it's true and very real to me. If the person of power and influence connects with your vision s(he) will ask you more questions and before you know it, s(he) will begin to connect you with the resources necessary to support your vision.

A note of *warning!* There are "**fake**" Elevator

Multipliers, "wannabe's," who pretend to know people and have influence but really need your talent, abilities, and personal power to help jump start their careers and/or lives! What warning signals and clues should you look for?

- They talk about themselves ALL the time!
- They are professional name droppers.
- They use the words "I" and "My" too often.
- They tend to live by their past successes.
- They are vision thieves looking for good ideas.
- They pursue money but not purpose.
- They don't keep their word. They lack integrity.
- They always "need" something from you.

If you want to maximize your life, seek Multipliers who are called to help you move from where you are to the place you'd rather be in life.[6] The key to having both Escalator and Elevator Multipliers in your life is that *you must be willing to take on the challenge to change, to think critically about your life, to face your realities, and to discover your personal power.*

Are you willing to change, to be challenged, to seek new levels of success? Multipliers expect that you will work harder, smarter, and wiser.

multipliers don't need you, you need them. They expect that given the opportunity, you will learn to lead yourself to new levels of success. Multipliers don't need you, you need them, so remember to thank them and honor them publicly whenever possible.

Who are the multipliers in your life? Who are the people who consistently provide you with opportunities to succeed in your life? Are any of the people from your Influential People list mul tipliers? Maybe this chapter has helped you identify multipliers in your life? If so, write down the names of the Multipliers and explain how they've multiplied your life. I also encourage you to send that person a card or note expressing thanks for multiplying your life. Interestingly, many people are Multipliers but they just don't know it! Your card or note will make their day, I assure you!

THE POWER OF PEOPLE

My Elevator Multipliers:

∞ _____

_____

∞ _____

_____

∞ _____

_____

How they multiply My Life?

∞ _____

_____

∞ _____

_____

∞ _____

_____

Are You A multiplier?

I challenge and encourage you to become a

Multiplier to someone else. Whose life can you help to jump start? Who have you been observing who has lots of potential, passion, and personal power but simply needs an opportunity? How can you provide escalator and elevator opportunities? If you have some ideas, write down their names; then start inquiring about their vision and purpose in life so that you can begin putting them on their escalators and elevators of success and personal power. Remember when we talked about "seed, time, and harvest" earlier? Well, being a Multiplier is like planting not just one seed but a field of seeds. The more you invest in others, the greater your harvest will be! *Your life will always benefit from multiplying someone else's life.*

Who will you multiply?

_____

_____

_____

_____

_____

_____

How will you multiply them?

_____

_____

_____

_____

_____

_____

---

[5] Ruiz, Miguel Angel (1997). The Four Agreements: A practical guide to personal freedom Needs. Amber-Allen Publishing, Inc. San Rafael, California

[6] Randy Morrison, pastor of Speak the Word Church International, Golden Valley, MN

Chapter 10

NOW, WHAT WILL YOU DO ABOUT THIS CONVERSATION?

I began this book with a short quote from Nelson Mandela, Nobel Peace prize winner, Apartheid war prisoner, first black South African President, father, husband, son, and man of great wisdom. Remember the quote:

"Our deepest fear is not that we are inadequate. Our deepest fear is that we are powerful beyond measure." That quote is only two lines of a longer one by then President Mandela. Let's finish the quote, for in it you will find great wisdom and powerful connections to the lessons you have learned in this book.[7]

"Our deepest fear is not that we are inadequate. Our deepest fear is that we are powerful beyond measure. It is our light, not our darkness, that most frightens us. We ask ourselves, who am I to be brilliant, gorgeous, talented, and fabulous? Actually, who are

you not to be? You are a child of God.
Your playing small doesn't serve the world. There's
nothing enlightened about shrinking so that other
people won't feel insecure around you. We are born
to manifest the glory of
God that is within us. It's not just in some
of us, it's in everyone. And as we let our
own light shine, we unconsciously give other
people permission to do the same. As we are
liberated from our own fear, our presence
automatically liberates others."

This quote elegantly points to the foundation
principle of this book, ***you are powerful.*** God
made you powerful, so stop pretending, acting,
and talking like you are not. Whether you like it
or not, you are a powerful person who can and
will directly affect people and situations around
you. A teenage keynote speaker put it this way,
"You are a self-contained grassroots revolution!"

Recently, as my son and I sat over breakfast
at a local restaurant, I was painfully reminded of
this power as a woman sitting next to us at the
counter began to reveal her story about powerful
parents. She spoke of her father, a powerful

Subtracter and Divider, who had continually belittled her and caused her to doubt her potential, her abilities, and her personal power. She was near tears as she shared examples of his power in her life. This 42-year-old woman was suffering from the powerful, but negative, words her father continued to speak to her.

My heart ached for this woman; then I literally became indignant! I quickly began teaching her about her personal power. I believe we were destined to meet because this woman was desperate to hear that she was indeed a powerful person who did not have to accept her father's negative words. She could choose the kind of life she wanted! She didn't have to settle for what her father said she was; she could begin to change her mind about herself and begin to discover her personal purpose and power.

So, what type of powerful person are you? Are you an Adder, Subtracter, Divider, or Multiplier? Have you chosen to be this type of powerful person or have you been socialized by your family, friends, or life circumstances to be this person? Do you know that your life experiences, with your family in particular, can create a false sense of self in you? Worse yet, we tend to become to others the person we most despised in our youth. So if you were raised by parents who were Subtracters, you grow up to be a Subtracter. Have you ever been around people who literally cannot find anything good to say about anything or anyone? It's as if their brains are stuck on negative!!

I once worked with a woman who had only experienced bosses who were Subtracters and Dividers. This woman's whole work and life perspective had to be adjusted because I would not tolerate negativity on my team! It was one of the most difficult assignments I have encountered. Daily, I Added to this woman. I worked hard on how to Multiply her life. What was I doing? I was teaching her how to think about herself as a confident, competent, and powerful person. This was painful and hard work for both of us. Sometimes I wanted to send her back to negative land but I knew I couldn't. I was sent into her life not to be her boss but to Add to her life and teach her to access her personal power.

- Am I asking you to be honest with yourself? Yes!

- Do I realize that these questions may be painful and uncomfortable? Yes!

- Do I understand that when you begin to realize your personal purpose and power that you might have to make some difficult decisions about the powerful negative people in your life? Yes!

- Do I understand that some of the people who supposedly care about you, may treat you badly, turn their backs on you, talk about you, accuse you of trying to be better than they are or even cuss you out? Yes!

Having gone through all of these stages, I have come to understand that the "no pain, no gain" fitness slogan is really true! As you discover your personal power and begin to use your power of Choice, you will experience pain! But this pain is only for a season! This season will end and soon you will begin to create a circle of powerful people who are Adders and Multipliers. Soon you will consciously become an Adder or Multiplier in someone else's life. Soon you will begin to discover your life's purpose and your personal power to succeed.

Now What?

This conversation is only the beginning. I expect that you will continue this conversation with your friends, colleagues, and family members. I hope that you take the wisdom from these pages and begin to teach and mentor others. People are looking for someone to help them rethink the meaning of life! People want to understand their power. As you discover your power and your purpose, don't keep it to yourself. Tell someone else your story. Begin to empower the lives of others by living a positive, powerful, and purposeful life. I know for a fact that someone in or around your life is waiting for you to discover your personal power and purpose! Start now by taking a moment to think about who you are, how you are, and how you want to affect the lives of others and your world! Here are a few questions to get you started:

> *someone in or around your life is waiting for you to discover your personal power and purpose!*

⚬ What are you passionate about in life?

⚬ _____

_____

⚬ What makes you angry enough or sad
   enough to motivate you to want to do
   something about it?

⚬ _____

_____

⚬ What are you good at? What do Adders
   typically complement you about?

⚬ _____

_____

⚬ When have you felt the most happy,
   fulfilled, and confident about who you
   are? What were you doing? How did you
   feel? Who were you being? Who were you
   with?

⚬ _____

_____

⚬ If you could be anything or do anything,
   what would it be?

∞ _____

_____

∞ If you could choose your parents, what
would they be like? Describe them.

∞ _____

_____

∞ If you could change one thing about
yourself or your life, what would it be?

∞ _____

_____

∞ Who are you most of the time when you
interact with others?
- ∞ Adder
- ∞ Subtracter
- ∞ Divider
- ∞ Multiplier

∞ _____

_____

∞ Who is in your inner circle? Who are the
people you talk to, trust, spend time with,
and ask for advice? What type of powerful

people are they? What type of powerful
person are you to them?

         ⬭ _____

            _____

         ⬭ _____

            _____

         ⬭ _____

            _____

⬭ After you have lived your life, what do
   you want others to say about you? What
   difference do you want to have made?
   What will be your legacy?

         ⬭ _____

            _____

What is the most powerful lesson you learned
from this book? What will you remember *and* act
on?

         ⬭ _____

            _____

My Hope For You

I believe in you, in your power, in your ability to positively change your world! May God bless you as you strive to discover the powerful person that you are. Don't let anyone or anything distract you from finding your personal power.

> Your power is in you, not in someone else.

Your power is in you, not in someone else. This is work that you have to do, for yourself! So get started and I guarantee that you will find great success in your life. You will never be the same!

Let me leave you with the Jabez Prayer. Jabez was a man whose name meant pain. He was surrounded by Subtracters and Dividers. He needed Adders and Multipliers so he prayed a powerful prayer in which he pleaded to God for *help!* My hope is that this prayer will motivate you to begin your journey to personal power and purpose.

NOW, WHAT WILL YOU DO ABOUT THIS CONVERSATION

"And Jabez called on the God of Israel saying,
Oh, that you would bless me indeed!
And enlarge my territory,
And that your hand would be with me,
And that you would keep me from evil,
So that I may not cause pain!
So God granted his request."

---

[7] IBID pp. 6

[8] 2001 National Service-Learning Conference, Denver, Colorado

[8] Your ability to influence your life powerfully and the lives of those around you is phenomenal.

[9] Wilkinson, Bruce (2000). The prayer of Jabez: Breaking Through to a Blessed Life. Multnomah Publishers, Inc. Based on Chronicles 4:9-10, The Holy Bible

Acknowledgments

I thank God for loving me, for giving me His wisdom, and for giving me His Son Jesus Christ. I am humbled that God would use me to teach and mentor others. I am also thankful for my family and particularly my children, Justice Cameron, Ktyal Liberty Amani, and Cornelius Scott for teaching me to always see the best in others, to think a new thought, to find reasons to laugh, and to be thankful for each new day of my life.

I offer my sincere thanks to my mentors and friends: Alice Journey, MA,L.P. who took me away for a weekend in the woods to let me write; Janie Westbrook, who always prays for me, inspires me, and has words of wisdom for my life; Paula Darkins, who is my constant cheerleader; Dr. Pamela Toole who believes in me, and encourages me, and reminds me of God's hand in my life, my editor, Laura Young, who believed in this project from its inception, and my publishing consultant, Tami Rangel, who worked diligently with me to make this book a reality.

Acknowledgments

I also want to thank the many friends, colleagues, family and pastors who were there to pray for and encourage me to pursue excellence in my life.

Thank you to my publishing team: Marilyn Alstrup, Tee Simmons and Tami Rangel for everything. You are an inspiration and blessing to my life.

Finally, a special thanks to all of the readers who took time out of your life to critically reflect on and review this book. Your words of wisdom, insights and challenging questions have helped to create a book that will genuinely help people understand their power.

Verna Cornelia Simmons, Ph.D.

2001

Contact Information:

C/O Verna Cornelia Simmons

JCAMA Publishers

Robbinsdale, MN 55422

www.jcama.com

Phone: 763-536-5975

Fax: 763-536-7881

email: missverna@jcama.com

---

[10] Empowerment Conference, May 2000, Speak the Word Church International, Golden Valley, MN

[11] IBID pp. 7

About the Author

Verna Cornelia Simmons is the president and principal consultant for J. Cameron & Associates, an organization committed to empowering and motivating people to realize and positively use their personal power. Verna Cornelia is an educator, entrepreneur, motivational speaker, author, personal coach, college professor and organizational consultant. Her professional experience includes work as a pre-school teacher, 5-6th grade teacher, program director, elementary school principal intern, senior marketing manager, assistant dean of women, director of leadership programs, and college professor. Verna Cornelia received her Ph.D. in Educational Policy and Administration

from the University of Minnesota where she is currently an adjunct professor. She is blessed to be the mother of Justice Cameron and the twins, Cornelius Scott and Ktyal Liberty Amani.